Reinhart Brandau

OUTSIDE THE DOOR
from
Three Bird-Moons

DA DRAUSSEN VOR DER TÜR
aus
Drei Vogelmonde

experienced and narrated
erlebt und erzählt

English and German
Englisch und Deutsch

and
photos
by
Reinhart Brandau

copyright 2012 by Reinhart Brandau

published by:
Herstellung und Verlag:
BoD Books on Demand www.bod.de
(Printmedium & e-Book)
ISBN 978-3-8482-2577-4

... this "Outside the Door" ... it´s so very different ...
and I´m longing to tell Wolfgang Borchert the whole story ...
and that´s what I do in spirit, again and again ...

... dieses so andere "Draußen vor der Tür" ...
wie gerne hätte ich Wolfgang Borchert davon erzählt! ...
und das ist es, was ich in Gedanken immer wieder tue ...

Unverhofft, wie eine Sternschnuppe aus dem Sternenmeer, fällt diese wirklich erlebte und vor allem wahre Vogelgeschichte ins Internet – eine der vielen Geschichten, die noch wie lauter Inseln in endloser Kette im mächtigen Strom der Zeit ruhn …

Als ich versuchte, sie wie einen Schatz aus dem Strom der Zeit in unsere Gegenwart zu heben, blieben einige Bilder der vorhergehenden Geschichte von dem kleinen Sperber auf den folgenden Seiten hängen – wobei sich das vollständige Sperberabenteuer inzwischen in dem "Papierbuch": „Drei Greifvögel" verborgen halt …

Unhoped for, like a shooting star falling from orbit, this real and above all true bird-tale drops into the internet, being one of those stories that remain, for the time being, like an endless chain of islands, in that mighty river of time …

When I began to raise it like a treasure out of this river of time into here and now, pictures of the little sparrow-hawk got stuk on some of the following pages, whereas the whole story of this remarkable bird is now hidden between the pages of the "paper-book": „Three Birds of Pray", for you to discover …

baden?　　　　bathing?

nach dem Bad, Gefiederpflege …   after bathing, grooming …

Traumflug   dream-fligh

in seine geheime Welt …   to its secret world …

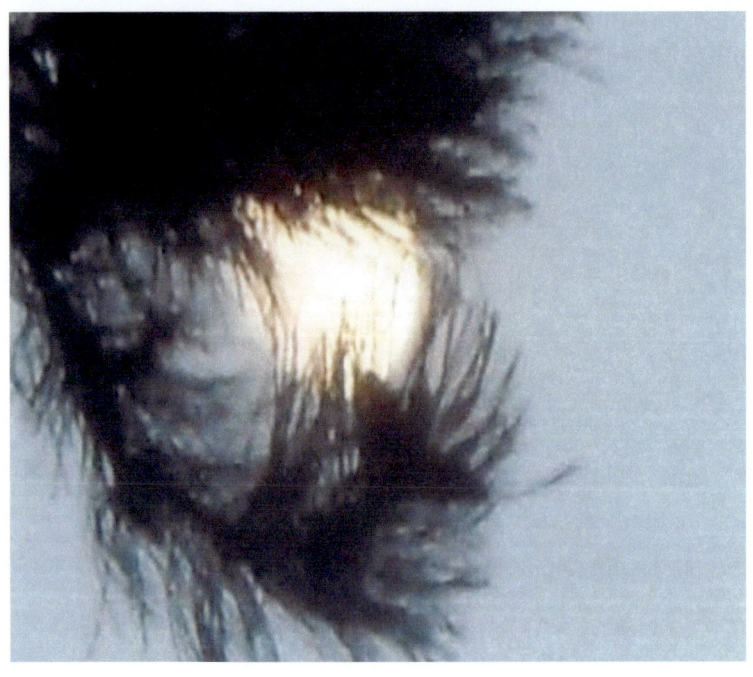

Drei Vogelmonde lang könnten die Vögel wohl bei mir sein, hab ich so gedacht, als die ersten Vogelkinder zu mir kamen – und nun?, der wievielte Mond wird dieser wohl sein? ...

The birds would stay round about three bird-moons, so I guessed, when the first baby-birds arrived – well, which moon may this one be now? …

und was wird der neue Tag wohl mit sich bringen?, Montag der 13. Juni 2011? …

what destiny may now be hidden in this new day?, Monday, June 13th 2011? …

DA DRAUSSEN VOR DER TÜR   OUTSIDE THE DOOR

ruft eine winzige Stimme   a tiny voice is calling
nach mir   me

unter den schützenden Zweigen
dieser Eibe, irgendwo im Immergrün verborgen –

hidden in evergreens somewhere
beneath the sheltering branches
of this yew-tree –

kleine Stimme führt mich zu
seinem Versteck

tiny voice is leading me to its
hiding-place

irgendwo da drinnen …   somewhere in there …

kein Zuhause mehr? … und nun? …
ersteinmal vorsichtig in die Hand
nehmen – zum Glück ist er noch
warm, einige Tropfen Wasser, weiße
Mehlwürmer, sachte lege ich ihn
zwischen die Pflanzen zurück und
hoffe auf irgendein Wunder …
das erscheint auch bald in Gestalt …

nicht nur mich hat die kleine
Vogelkinderstimme gerührt, auch
der Vogelpapa folgt ihrem Klang,
begrüßt sein verlorenes Kind leise:
tok, tok, tok, leise, daß kein Feind
sie bemerkt, leise wie ein heimliches
Versprechen, fliegt zum Waldrand,
wo er im Laub nach Eßbarem sucht,

no home any more? … and what shall
we do now? … taking him carefully
in my hand, I feel he is still warm all-
right – some drops of water, white
mealworms, then I lay him back carefully between the sheltering plants
hoping for a miracle …
that soon appears in the shape of …

it´s not only me, the birds tiny voice
has touched deeply – the birds daddy,
following its sound, is now greeting
his lost child softly: tok, tok, tok, low-
voiced so no enemy will be aware of
them, softly, like a secret promise and
flys to the edge of the wood where he
looks for food beneath moist foliage,

eilt mit Würmern im Schnabel zu	hurrying back to our baby-bird,
unserem Vogelkind zurück – tok,	worms in beak, tok, tok, tok,
tok, tok, ganz leise – Papa ist da …	very softly – daddy´s back …

Freudentränen?, was auch immer –
rinnen einfach so …

erst wußte ich ja nicht wieso das noch
halbnackte Vogelbaby aus dem Nest,
oben in der Eibe, herabgefallen ist –
dann berichtete mir Annette von wü-
tendem Geschimpfe der Amseleltern
am Morgen, und daß sie von ihrem
Fenster aus in ein zerstörtes, leeres
Nest blickt … neben Annettes Stimme
nun noch eine kleine, leise Vogelstimme – kalte zwölf Grad ist es nur; lege
die Kinder zueinander – und wärmen
sich ein wenig aneinander …

tears of happiness?, what so ever – just
simply falling …

up to this point I don´t yet know why
this almost naked baby-bird has fallen
down from its nest, way up in the yew-
tree – then Annette tells me of angry
blackbirds that have been shouting at
some one she couldn´t make out and
that she is now looking into a destroyed empty nest … besides Annettes
voice I now hear another, tiny bird-
voice – it is cold, only twelve degr-
ees – I lay the baby-birds together –
they keep each other warm a bit …

glücklich ist mein Amselfreund –
versorgt unsere Kinder mit Regenwürmern, die er unter feuchtem
Laub findet und weißen Mehlwürmern,
die er von mir bekommt – in den Pausen
singt er sein Glücklichsein in die Welt …
Mama Amsel jedoch ist völlig durch
den Wind – traut sich nicht her, irrt
jammernd und klagend am Waldrand
umher, und tut mir in der Seele leid …

derweil versuche ich die Ärmste so
weit ich kann zu ersetzen, ihrem
Gefährten zu helfen die Kleinen zu
versorgen, und den Kindern ein guter
Hilfspapa zu sein …

neben all der Lebendkost bereite ich
ihnen noch leckere Eigelb-Quark-
Haferkleiebällchen zu, die ich ihnen
zwischendurch mit ein paar Tropfen
Wasser in die Schnäbel gebe –

wo es nun doch zwei sind, kann ich ja
immer mal eins unserer Kinder zum
aufwärmen im Badezimmer unter
die Wärmelampe legen – mit nur
einem hungrigen Schnabel wird der
Amselpapa zur Not wohl auch
zufrieden sein – hat bestimmt eins
seiner Kinder genauso lieb wie zwei,
wie ich ja auch …

happily, my blackbird-friend – treating
our children with earthworms, he is
collecting under the moist foliage, and
white mealworms, which I supply for
him – during pauses he is singing his
happiness to the world … mother
blackbird though is just out of her wits –
doesn´t dare come near, going astray
along the edge of the woods mourning
in misery – pity her with all my soul …

meanwhile I just try to take the place of
the poor mother-bird, as well as I can, to
help her husband raise the little ones
and to be as good an auxiliary-dad as
can be …

apart from all that living food I prepare
for them delicious white-cheese, cooked
egg-yolk, flaked oats-balls which
I ´ll give them in between, adding some
drops of water, into their beaks –

they now being two children, it will be
all right if I lay one of them at a time
in the bathroom under the infrared lamp,
since one hungry beak will surely make
father blackbird just as happy as two of
them – he will love one of his children
just as much as two, just as I do …

wenn aber eines mal weiterkrabbelt –	imagining, one of them creeping off –
zum Weg,	onto the path,

und es kommt wer daher und	where someone will come along and
tritt … nein!	step … oh no!

versperre mal schnell den Weg;	will close the way right now;
KEIN ZUGANG!	NO ENTERY!
VOGELKINDER ZU FUSS!	CHILDREN-BIRDS WALKING!
und: Post bitte in Tüte, danke!	and: mail in bag please, thank you!

die Welt soll
draußen bleiben!,
ein geschützter
Ort! – und mir
dämmert – habe
soeben die Pforte
zum Paradies
hinter uns
geschlossen …

the world shall
stay outside!,
a sheltered sanc-
tuary – slowly
getting aware of
just having clo-
sed the gate to
Paradise behind
us …

nun hört es sich an, wie eine ganz, ganz
kleine Vogelstimme – von unterm
Briefkasten her – zu sehen ist jedoch
nur Pflanzengrün …

now it sounds like a very, very
tiny bird´s-voice – from beneath
the mail-box – yet, except for
green foliage, no living thing can
I spot …

18

doch meine Finger berühren Weiches,
nicht mehr sehr Warmes, das sich
festkrallt und aus ängstlichen Augen zu
mir aufschaut als ich seine Krallenfinger
vorsichtig von ihrem Halt löse und das
hilflose Geschöpf zu seinem Geschwis-
terchen unter die Wärmelampe lege …

oh!, my fingers are touching something
soft, it is not very warm any more, its
claws clutching some greenery, looking
up at me with fearful eyes as I carefully
loosen its claw-fingers from their hold,
bringing the helpless creature to its little
brother or sister to the warm-lamp …

unsere Vogelkinder bekommen die leck-
eren Klößchen von mir nur auf dem Weg
zur Wärmelampe damit sie, wenn ich
sie ihrem leiblichen Papa zurückbringe,
für sein Würmerangebot wieder Platz
in ihrem Bäuchlein haben – Regenwürmer sucht er natürlich selbst, Mehlwürmer bekommt er dann von mir –

our bird-children are getting those delicious balls from me only when I take
them to the warm-lamp, so, bringing
them back to their real dad, there might
be sufficient space in their little bellies
for all those earthworms he will offer
them – those he collects at the edge
of the forest, mealworms I deliver to

und hat absolutes Vertrauen zu seinem federlosen Freund, der alles darf,
sogar seine Kinder umher zu tragen
erlaubt er ihm; ganz in seiner Welt
zu sein … Urvertrauen, endlich ange-

kommen … hier auf Erden … im
Pradies

him – and there is total confidence
into his featherless friend, who may do
anything, allows me even to carry
around his children, to be in his world
completely, in absolute confidence …

at last we arrived, here on this planet …
in paradise …

Verlassenes Amselnest – genau das
richtige!, denke ich, lege alle unsere
Kleinen hinein …

Abandoned blackbirds-nest – just the
right thing!, I guess, putting all our
children in …

Amselpapa schaut es sich genau an …   blackbird-dad inspecting …

und füttert auch im fremden Nest   feeds although this is an unknown nest

Es ist kalt – grau verhangener Himmel; und wird wohl bald auch noch regnen – mein schwarzer Freund hat unsere Kinder so alle halbe Stunde mit irdischer Kost versorgt, dann, wenn er nicht auf Futtersuche unterwegs war, hat er für uns und alle deren Seelen nicht verschüttet sind Freude und Glücklichsein in die Welt gesungen – nun, der Abend dämmert schon herein, stimmt er sein nicht enden wollendes Gutenachtlied an das erst in tiefer Nacht verklingen wird ... drei kleine Amseln, geborgen am Erdboden, hat es wohl noch nie gegeben – und geborgen?, na ja, solange ich sie bewache schon; und das tue ich den lieben langen Tag – doch des Nachts – wenn arglistig umherschleichende Krallenpfoten unterwegs sind ... mitsamt ihrem neuen Zuhause bringe ich unsere Kinder in's Badezimmer, wo ich ihr Nest in die nur ganz mild wärmende Peripherie des Rotlichts lege ...

It´s cold today – grey sky above – may be it will be raining soon ... round about every half an hour, my black friend provides our children with earthly food after which, if he was n´t engaged in collecting food, for us, and all whose souls haven´t been buried yet, he would sing his happiness and love into this world – now, as dusk closes in, he begins his endless lullaby – not before deep in the night will it die away ... three baby-blackbirds, sheltered in their nest on the ground, such never happend before, I believe, and sheltered?, indeed, as long as I watch over them which I do all through the day – but at night, when malicious creeping claw-paws will be around ... huddled in their nest, our baby-birds, I´ll take them with their nest to the bathroom and place them into the very milde-warm periphery of the warm-lamp ...

Dienstag 14. Juni 4°° – Gesang vieler Vogelstimmen weckt mich aus leichtem Schlaf – 6°°, krabbel unter warmen Decken hervor, schlurfe in Hausschuhen zu meinen Vogelkindern in´s Badezimmer, nehme das Nest mit ihnen hoch und vor die Tür, vor der ihr Vogelpapa mit dem Schnabel voller Regenwürmer auf uns wartet … hier sind deine Kinder – lege das Nest in eine kleine Erdmulde – und wie ich es noch zurechtrücke ist der Papa schon bei seinen Kindern …

unser Paradies hat seine Pforten wieder für uns aufgetan …

Tuesday, June 14th 4 a.m. – the singing of all those birds wakes me up from shallow sleep – 6 a.m., scramble from under warm blankets, shuffle with slippers into the bathroom where I take my children-birds up with their nest and step outside where their papa-bird is awaiting us, with earthworms in his beak … here are your children – and, while I place the nest into the little earth-mould, papa-bird has already come to his children …

our paradise again has opened its gates for us …

nach dem Frühstück stellt sich sogleich die Frage: „ seid ihr denn immer noch nicht satt?" …

right after having had their breakfast; one is inclined to ask: „you aren´t asking for more, are you?" …

als ich mir dann zu meinem Frühstück Tee einschenken will, schaut mich ein Heupferd vom Rand meiner Teeschale her an …Tee kann warten …

about to pour tea for breakfast into my teacup, a grasshopper looks at me from the rim of that cup …

tea may wait …

dieses grasgrüne Geschöpf betrachtet
mich aufmerksam, setzt über das
Spülbecken mit perfekter Landung
auf dem Rand einer Tonschale die es
mit den Füßen seiner beiden Sprung-
beine und der vier anderen Beine
eingehend befühlt – wie lauter eigen-
ständige Lebewesen kommen mir
diese schlanken, gelenkigen, alle Un-
ebenheiten ausgleichenden Glied-
maßen vor – schwupp – Sprung auf
den Boden einer Bratpfanne, die an
der Wand hängt – glatt und mit Über-
hang – klettert bedächtig aufwärts –
wie ein Bergsteiger, doch ohne Eisen,
Haken und Ösen … schenke mir
endlich meinen Tee ein …

this grass-green creature, seeming to
inspect me curiously, now jumps across
the wash-basin with perfect landing on
the rim of an earthenware-bowl which it
touches investigating with the feet of its
jumping legs as well as the other four –
all its legs seem to be selfreliant living
creatures, these slender, pliable, limbs –
schwupp … jumping on the back of a
frying-pan which hangs on the wall –
slippery, overhanging –
the grasshopper is climbing upwards,
deliberately like a mountaineer,
and does´nt need any equipment at all …

so I ´ll poor myself tea, in that now
abandoned cup …

Schwüle – kündigt Gewitter an – oder
schlimmeres …

hab gesehn, wie Vögel sich auf ihre
Kinder legten und ihre Flügel schirmend
über sie breiteten, als es zu regnen
begann …

wenn es bald regnet, womöglich heftiger
Regen auf die nackten Kleinen nieder-
prasselt … und auf die Erdhummeln, die
unter dem Rost vor der Haustür ihr Zuhause eingerichtet haben … schnell, der
kleine runde Gartentisch als Regendach
über die Kinderstube – und wenn unser
Amselpapa den Tisch bedrohlich findet,
und sich nicht mehr zu seinen Kindern
traut? – vorsichtshalber stell ich den
Regendachtisch erstmal nur neben das
Nest unter die Eibe … als Papa mit dem
Schnabel voll Regenwürmern wieder
unter die Eibenzweige zu seinen Kindern
huscht, scheint er den Gartentisch nicht
zu beachten, hat nur seine hungrigen
Kinder im Sinn .. was für ein Vogel-
Vater! …

stifling – foreboding thunderstorm – or
worse …

I have seen birds lay down upon their
little ones, sheltering them by spreading
their wings over them, when heavy rain
was falling …

in case, maybe soon, severe rain will
pour down on the naked little birds as
well as on the bumble-bees, which
have built their home beneath the grating in front of the door … I will put
the little garden-table sheltering over
the nursery – but what, if blackbird-dad
thinks the table is threatening, and
does´nt dare look after his children any
more? – precautiously I put the rain-
shelter-table for the time being beside
the nest under the yew-tree … when dad,
earthworms in his beak, again whisks
under the yew-tree-branches to his
children he does n´t seem to take any
notice of the garden-table … just caring
for his hungry children, he doesn´t seem
to bother at all …

finster der Himmel – stelle den Gartentisch getrost über die Kinderstube, noch
ein Regenschutzbrett darüber und werde

gloomy sky above – now I`ll place
the garden-table unhesitatingly over
the nursery adding a sheltering board

sie auch noch mit Rhododendronblätter-
werk gegen Feindesaugen tarnen – kann
sie außerdem immernoch reinholen wenn´s
zu schlimm wird: Taifun oder so –

and some small rhododendron-branches,
to screen the little ones from the sight
of foes – in case of typhoon, or such
like, I can take them in any way –

natürlich hat Papa Amsel seine Kinder

nicht lange suchen müssen …

of course daddy-blackbird recognises

his children instantly …

unsere Vogelkinder sind nun ja für
alle Wetter unter Tisch und Baum –
doch unter dem Rost …

die Erdhummelkinder – Königin –
Väter, Mütter, Arbeiter oder was
es bei ihnen so alles gibt – weiß es
ja auch nicht, war noch nie in einem
Hummelheim –

now our bird-children are sheltered
all right beneath table and tree – but
under the grating …

the bumlebee-children – queen –
dads, mothers, workers, whatever
inhabitants there are – obviously, I
do´nt know, I´ve never been inside
bumblebee-homes –

welche Hummelwesen es auch immer
sind, auch sie sollen nicht naß werden – schon gar nicht ertrinken …

whatever kind of bumble-creatures they
may be, they won´t get wet either – and
for shure, they will not drown …

seine Kinder unter sich, begrüßt er
blitzezuckendes Donnern und Regenrau-
schen mit leidenschaftlichem Gesang …

his children below him, he is greeting
thunder and lightning and the rushing
rain with his song …

auch im bedrohlichen Spiel dieser
Naturgewalten gibt es für ihn nur
Freude und Glücklichsein über seine
Kinder, und unser hier und jetzt
Paradies …
mir hat sein Lied Freude und Glück-
lichsein geschenkt; und das Gefühl
daß wir alle zusammen eine große
Familie sind – und natürlich gehö-
en auch die Meisen dazu, und die
Finken, und die Ringeltauben, die
sogar lesen können und glauben, daß

inspite of the threatening game of these
natural powers, he is ever so happy
beholding his children, and our
here and now paradise …

his song just made me happy, made me
be aware of all of us together being just
one happy family – including the great-
tits, and the finches, and the doves,
who, having read the message on the
chair: NO ENTRY, do believe it is
meant for them and do not dare pass

das Gebot an der Lehne des kleinen
Stuhles: KEIN ZUTRITT, ihnen gilt,
und trauen sich nicht mehr, wie ehedem,
zu uns hereinzuspazieren, in unsere
friedvolle kleine Welt …

the chair into our peaceful little world …

solange die Kleinen ihr Nest noch nicht
verlassen haben, dürfen diese dicken,
schweren Vögel auch nicht Gelegenheit
bekommen, wenn auch nur versehentlich,
über unsere Kinderstube zu stolpern, sich
zu erschrecken und bei dem dann unver-
meidlichen Blitzstart die Kinder ernstlich
zu verletzen – streue ihnen ihre Sonnen-
blumenkerne nun vor den Stuhl auf den
Weg …

while the little ones will stay in their
nest, I won´t allow those big, heavy
birds to linger around there where
they might stumble across the little
birds in their nest, and, getting start-
led, hurt them with their big feet in
their take-off – so, from now on, I
strew the pealed sunflower-seeds for
them in front of the chair on the
path …

… aus heiterem Himmel greift eine schwarze Knochenhand mir ans Herz – unverhofft erschüttern die Umtriebe eines Krallenpfotenwesens die Grundfesten unseres kleinen Paradieses …

… descending from a blue sky, a black bony-hand clutches my heart – unhoped-for, subversive activities by a claw-paw-creature are shaking our little paradise to its very foundations …

schmerzdurchwühlt zitternd hockt er vor sich hin … der Vogel …

this bird, which a lady has brought to me, is crouching, pain-shaken quivering, amidst fading life …

am Morgen noch treusorgender Kleiberpapa … nun sterbendes

having tended its little ones even this morning … now this claw-paws-horror

Krallenpfotengrauen in meiner Hand …   dying in my hand …

drücken sich in's Nest, daß sie ja kein
Feind entdeckt – danke für heiles Leben …

crouching, hoping that no enemy will notice
them – thanks for sound life …

Dank dem Papa der sie so
liebevoll betreut …

thanks to their dad for looking
after them so tenderly …

der, wenn er sie mit weltlicher Kost
versorgt hat, ihnen in seinem Gesang
von Leben und Liebe erzählt …

he, who, after having fed them with
worldly food is telling them of life
and love by his song …

dann, gegen 20°°, nach dem Abend-
mahl, beginnt Papa Amsel das vielleicht
hingebungsvollste, schönste, das Gute-
nachtlied zu singen – bis in die tiefe
Dämmerung hinein …
dann könnte ich die Kinder schon für
die Nacht reinholen – ihr Papa würde
sie sicher nicht vermissen, hat sich
doch ganz in seinen Gesang vertieft –

finally, about 8 p.m., after supper, pa
blackbird will begin to chant the most
devoted, most beautiful lullaby for his
love, hiding in the forest, and his chil-
dren all through the dusk into the dee-
pening night … then, I could take our
children in for the night – sure, daddy
would not miss them, getting lost in
his singing by now – but the little ones

aber die Kleinen lauschen seiner Zauber-
stimme mit mir; daß ihr Klingen uns zur
Nacht in wundersame Träume geleiten
wird …

will listen to his enchanting voice together with me, while its sound will lead
us to wondrous dreaming at night …

Mittwoch 15. Juni 6°°
vor der Haustür gleitet etwas schwarzes
in der Eibe herab zum Nest und begrüßt
leise, tok, tok, tok seine Kinder; und
meine Hände welche die Kinderstube in
ihre Erdmulde betten …
scheuer Vogel, nach wie vor, immer auf
der Hut – extrem wachsam, hört und sieht
alles und huscht in Deckung, gedanken-

Wednesday June 15th 6°° a.m.
in front of the backdoor a black shape
descends down the yew-tree to the nest
greeting its children softly, tok, tok, tok,
as well as my hands, while they are
placing the nest into the earth-mould …
very shy, father blackbird, after all, ever
keen on his guard, watchful ears and
eyes, the faintest sign of threatening

schnell, beim geringsten Anzeichen einer
drohenden Gefahr wobei er , mit geschloss-
enem Schnabel, einen hohen Warnton ruft …

danger causing him slip like lightning
under closest shelter calling a high
pitched warning, keeping his beak shut …

sobald jedoch ein Mensch in Sicht- oder
Hörweite kommt, sucht er schimpfend
das Weite – und ich, was bin ich in seinen Augen?, eine Ersatzvogelmama?, die
echte ist ja so traumatisiert daß sie sich
noch immer nicht in die Umgebung des
erlittenen Schreckens, zu ihren Kindern,
traut, daß ich an ihrer Stelle ihre Kinder
umsorge … für was auch immer Papa
Amsel mich hält – grenzenloses Vertrauen wie bedingungsloses Miteinander
verbinden uns …

if a human being comes in sight he das-
hes off, upset scolding, and me … what
does he think I am?, a substitude bird-
mama? – poor true bird-ma has obviously been shocked so badly, when some enemy destroyed the nest, and scattered her
babies all about the home-tree, that she
dares not return to the surroundings of
the terrifying attack of late – poor ma
does not dare return to her children,
which in the meantime I look after …
whatever papa blackbird thinks I am …
boundless confidence is uniting us …

fast ebenso notwendig wie gute Ernährung ist die Entsorgung – wie auch die Meisenbabies produzieren unsere Kleinen kunstvoll verpackte Kotballen; schneeweiß, mit einem dunkelbraunen schnabelgerechten Tragegriff – Vogelvater wartet auf dessen Erscheinen um ihn weit weg zu tragen, damit er keinem Feind die Kinderstube verraten wird …

as well as proper nourishment proper cleanliness is necessary – like the great-tit babies, our little ones too produce cleanly enclosed droppings; snow-white, furnished with a brown beakhold – father-bird waiting for these droppings, to carry them far away, so they will not give hints to lurking foes …

Donnerstag 16. Juni 7°°
hab doch glatt verschlafen – Papa erwartet uns, wie gewohnt, vor der Haustür; aber nicht wie man erwarten könnte, mit Geschimpfe, weil wir so spät dran sind – aus der Eibe begrüßt er uns mit einem fröhlichen Morgenlied …

Thursday June 16th 7°° a.m.
overslept – pa, as usual, awaiting us in the yew-tree, but not, as one could expect; scolding me for being late – he´s greeting us happily with his early morning song …

Mama Amsel hat sich nur bis auf den Weg herangetraut, und lauscht der geliebten Stimme ihres Gefährten; abgrundtief muß ihre Furcht vor dem Unheimlichen sein, der über sie und ihre Kinder hergefallen ist, ihr Heim zerstört, und eines ihrer Kinder verschleppt hat …

ah!, mama blackbird dares leave her exile in the woods, coming as near as the path behind the yew-tree, listening to the beloved voice of her husband … seems to be still terrified by what she has experienced, when some sinister creature fell upon her and her children, destroying their home and carrying off one of her little ones …

vielleicht, vielleicht – ich wünsche ihr so sehr daß sie ihre Kinder wiederfindet …

perhaps – I do wish with all my heart she may find her way back to her children …

in der Küche hab ich eben das Heupferd
wiedergefunden … es geht ihm nicht gut –
dankbar sieht es mich an, als ich es draußen
vorsichtig auf ein grünes Blatt setze … so
fühlt es sich an … jedenfalls …

I just discovered the grasshopper in the
kitchen again … it does´nt seem well …
looking at me expressing thankfulnes,
it seems, when I carefully place it upon
a green leaf outdoors …

Auge eines Freundes berührt mein Herz …   the eye of a friend touches my heart …

und das eines Flugwesens, eines der ganz, ganz wenigen der Maisfeldnervengiftkriegüberlebenden, das mich am Abend besucht – lese gerade in dem wunderbaren (mega geilen) Buch: DIE FARM IN DEN GRÜNEN BERGEN, von Alice Herdan-Zuckmayer …

as well as the eye of this little flying creature; one of those very, very few survivours of that deadly cornfield-nerve-gas-war, popping in at night, while I am reading in that marvellous (mega hot) book: THE FARM IN THE GREEN MOUNTAINS, by Alice Herdan-Zuckmayer …

18. Juni, ob Papa Amsel wohl weiß …   June 18th, does papa blackbird know …

… daß gleich eines unsrer Kinder nicht mehr im Nest zu finden sein wird? … daß ich auf allen Vieren unter der Eibe herumkriechen, und das verlorengegangene Vogelkind vergeblich suchen werde? … daß bald darauf das nächste, gefolgt von dem letzten aus dem Nest über das Immergrün in den Wald hüpft, daß ich ratlos in das leere Nest schau, und irgendwie so gar nicht weiterweiß? … Mama Amsel aber, die immer nur im Wald umherfliegend mit schriller Stimme lamentiert hat, hört sich nun sanft und sehr glücklich an … und traut sich endlich wieder unter die Eibe, wo nun auch sie von mir Würmer für ihre Kinder bekommt …

… that one of our children will soon leave the nest? … that I will creep on my hands and knees under the yew-tree in vain trying to recover the lost child-bird? … that soon the next one, and the third will leave the nest, hopping across the evergreen into the woods, leaving me puzzled, looking into the abandoned nest, not knowing what to do about all this … mama blackbird however, after roaming about in the woods lamenting with a piercing voice now calls softly, and like a very, very happy mother-bird … and even dares come again to the Yew-tree, where she picks up worms for her children …

… wer nun aber, wie ich ja auch, glaubt, sie währen ja inzwischen schon Jahre, die Vogelerlebnisse seien nun erstmal zuende, hat die Rechnung natürlich ohne die Vögel gemacht … bereits am 5. Juli fallen in Bremen zwei kleine Mehlschwalben mit einem Teil ihres Nestes auf einen Balkon hinab, und in meine Obhut – sie bilden die Vorhut der noch folgenden kleinen Vogelinvasion …

… anyone, like me, expecting the adventures with birds have now ended, is very mistaken …

as soon as June 5th, in the city of Bremen two little house-martins will, together with fragments of their nest, tumble down onto a balcony and into my care, being the vanguard of the following little bird-invasion …

… und … großes Indianerehrenwort – bin bereits dabei auch die nun folgenden Schwalbengeschichten aufzuschreiben, und ebenfalls als gebundenes Buch, wie auch als e-book, zu veröffentlichen …

… and … on my word of honour – am writing already the now following swallow-stories, for to publish them as a hardcover-book, as well as an e-book in internet …

doch alles braucht seine Zeit – leider …

it will take some time yet – alas! …

… so müssen auch wir, wie diese Spinne
auf Beute, geduldig auf das Erscheinen
der Schwalbengeschichten warten …

… so we too will have to wait patiently,
like this spider for its prey, for the
editing of the swallow-stories …

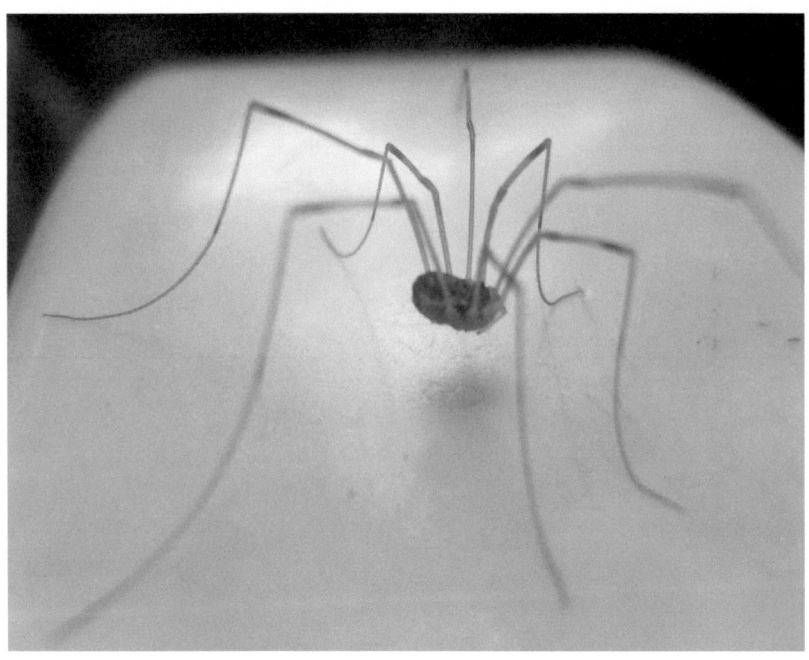

werden wir uns dann bald bei den
Schwalben wiedersehen? …

shall we soon meet again with the
swallows then? …

I really had forgotten that I was born once upon a time; as it happened a long time ago – and it was, perhaps, on January 14th, in the year 1936 …

In a tiny village, on the banks of the Schwarza in the Thuringian Forest – on the banks of this mysterious river that tells wonderous tales to those who understand the language of water, and listen to its voices: the roar under the waterfall, telling of life coming into being, of passing time, and eternity – the mysterious murmuring, when it rushes in gorges, its gay babble and promising tinkle as it plays with small stones –

And while this river drifts calmly along a deep bed, listening to the birds voices and the humming-whirringflying-songs of those small, winged creatures as they dance self- forgetting over the still water, if I then look down into the depths, from which low subterranean singing of a waterspirit floats up to me, I get moved by longing to be down there, and by strange sadness …

Close to the Schwarza I opened my eyes to the world, and it was there, where I left my childhood when the end of the war drove my little destiny-boat to Bremen where it lost its way until Mecki, the hooded crow, stopped it and led it to the birds world – where it dropped anchor at last …

Daß ich irgendwann mal geboren wurde, hatte ich schon ganz vergessen – ist ja auch so lange her – am 14. Januar könnte es gewesen sein, 1936 … in einem klitzekleinen Dorf am Ufer der Schwarza, mitten im Thüringer Wald – an dem geheimnisvollen Fluß der einem so wundersame Geschichten erzählt – wenn man die Sprache des Wassers versteht, und seinen Stimmen lauscht: dem Donnerrauschen unterm Wasserfall, das von der Entstehung des Lebens, der vorübereilenden Zeit und der Ewigkeit erzählt – dem geheimnisvollen Murmeln, wenn es durch felsige Engpässe eilt; seinem lustigen Klingen, wo es mit kleinen Steinen spielt –

Und wenn dieser Fluß in tiefem Bett still dahintreibt, den Stimmen der Vögel lauscht und sirrend-summendem Fluggesang kleiner Flügelwesen; die wie selbstvergessen über das ruhige Wasser tanzen, wenn ich dann in die Tiefe schau, aus der leiser Undinengesang zu mir heraufschwebt, ergreift mich Sehnsucht nach dort unten, und eine seltsame Traurigkeit …

Ganz nah der Schwarza hab ich das "Licht der Welt" erblickt, und dort meine Kindheit zurückgelassen, als das Kriegsende mein Lebensschiffchen nach Bremen verschlug, von wo es durch's Leben irrte bis Mecki, die Nebelkrähe, es anhielt, und in die Welt der Vögel geleitete – in der es endlich vor Anker ging …

As I thank fortune for having allowed me to aid so many birds in distress, and to be touched and moved by their spirit, I thank the commune of Worpswede, represented by Mr. Kranz, Mrs. Maas and Mrs. Uhlenwinkel, for having supported me in times of need …

So, wie ich dem Schicksal dafür danke, daß es mir immer wieder erlaubt hat in Not geratenen Vögeln zu helfen, und sie zu erleben, danke ich der Gemeinde Worpswede, daß sie, namentlich Herr Kranz, Frau Maas und Frau Uhlenwinkel, mich in einer Kriese so hilfreich unterstützt hat …